LEROY ANDERSON

Featuring "Blue Tango," "Sleigh Ride,"
"The Syncopated Clock" and many more!

Arranged by JOHN BRIMHALL

C O N T E N T S

Project Manager: Tony Esposito
Cover Design: Michael Ramsay

© 1999 WARNER BROS. PUBLICATIONS
All Rights Reserved

BLUE TANGO

Arranged by
JOHN BRIMHALL

Music by
LEROY ANDERSON

Tango tempo

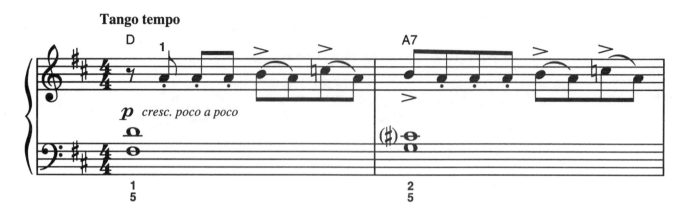

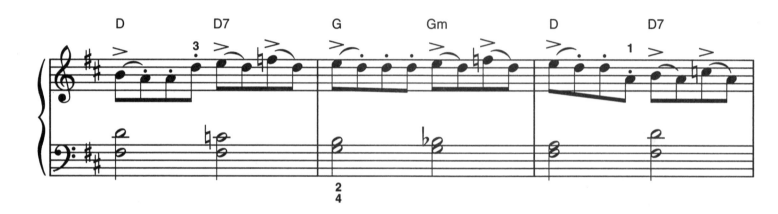

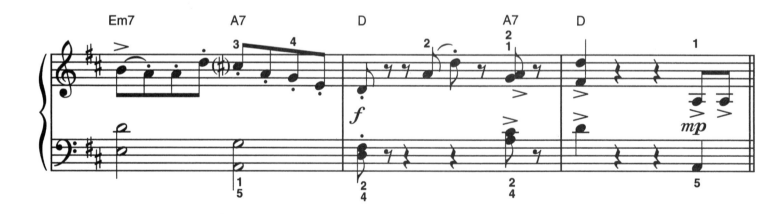

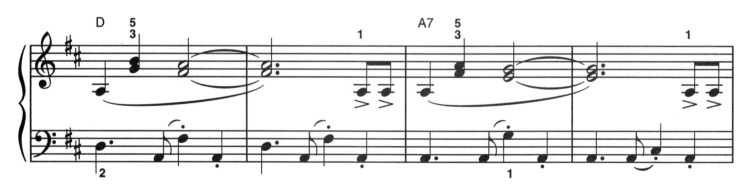

Blue Tango - 5 - 1

4

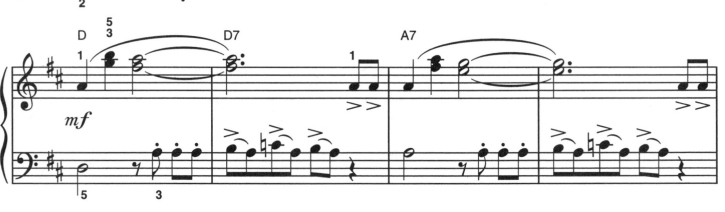

6

SLEIGH RIDE

Arranged by
JOHN BRIMHALL

Words by MITCHELL PARISH
Music by LEROY ANDERSON

Sleigh Ride - 5 - 1

Let's look at the show, We're rid-ing in a won-der-land of

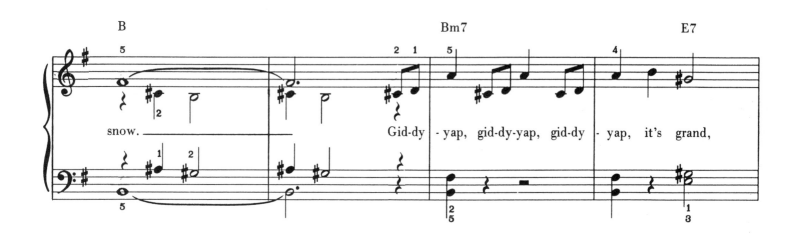

snow. _____ Gid-dy-yap, gid-dy-yap, gid-dy-yap, it's grand,

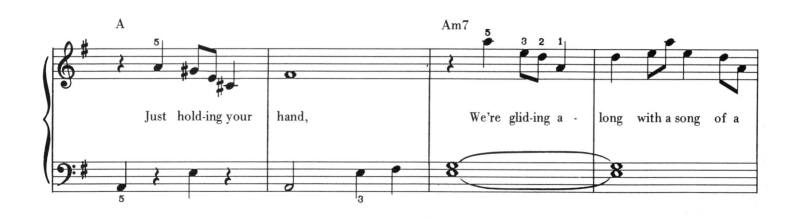

Just hold-ing your hand, We're glid-ing a-long with a song of a

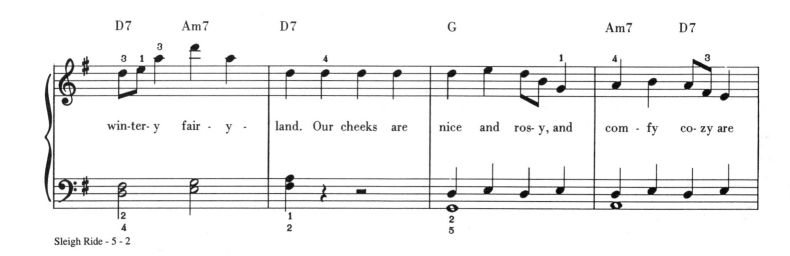

win-ter-y fair-y-land. Our cheeks are nice and ros-y, and com-fy co-zy are

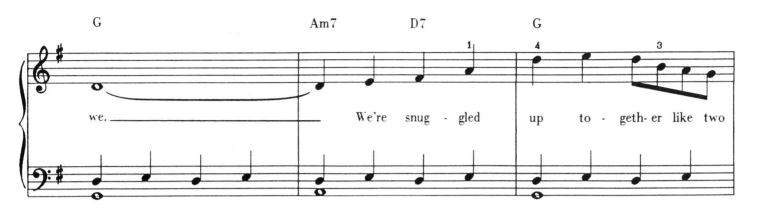

We. We're snug - gled up to - geth- er like two

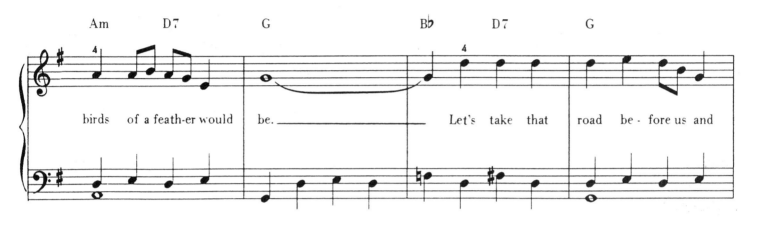

birds of a feath-er would be. Let's take that road be - fore us and

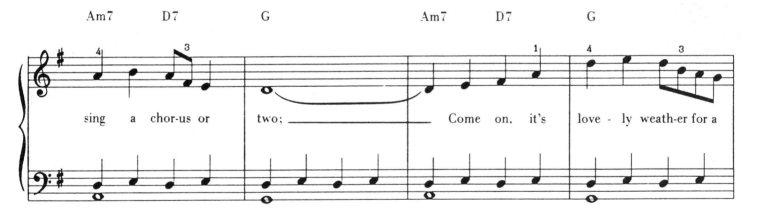

sing a chor-us or two; Come on, it's love - ly weath-er for a

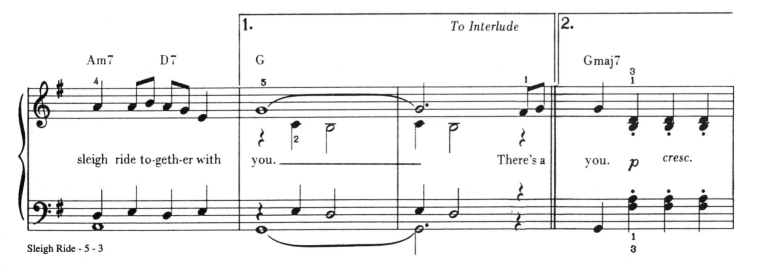

sleigh ride to-geth-er with you. There's a you.

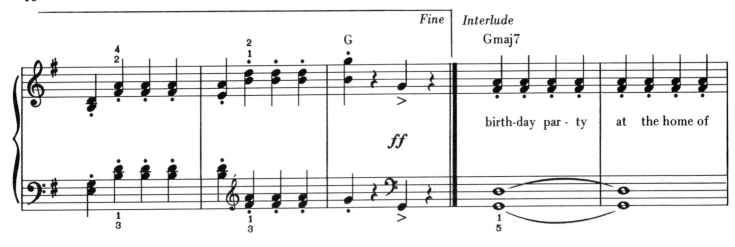

Fine | *Interlude*

birth-day par - ty at the home of

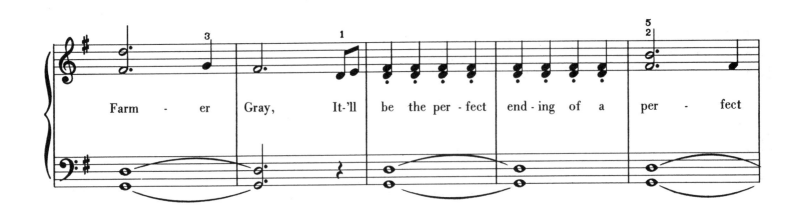

Farm - er Gray, It-'ll be the per - fect end - ing of a per - fect

day, we'll be sing-ing the songs we love to sing with - out a sin - gle

stop, At the fire - place while we watch the chest - nuts pop.

Sleigh Ride - 5 - 4

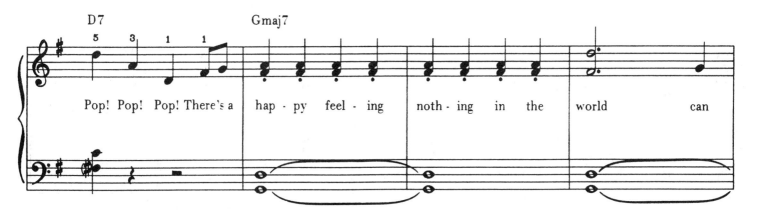

Pop! Pop! Pop! There's a hap - py feel - ing noth - ing in the world can

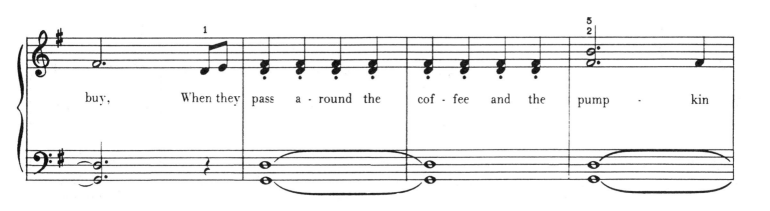

buy, When they pass a - round the cof - fee and the pump - kin

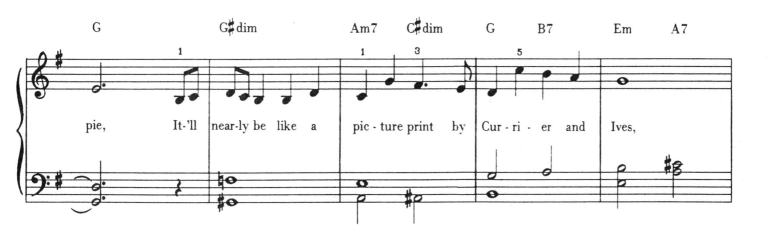

pie, It-'ll near-ly be like a pic - ture print by Cur - ri - er and Ives,

these won-der-ful days are the things we re- mem-ber all thru our lives! Just hear those

D.S. al Fine

Sleigh Ride - 5 - 5

THE SYNCOPATED CLOCK

Arranged by
JOHN BRIMHALL

Music by
LEROY ANDERSON

The Syncopated Clock - 4 - 1

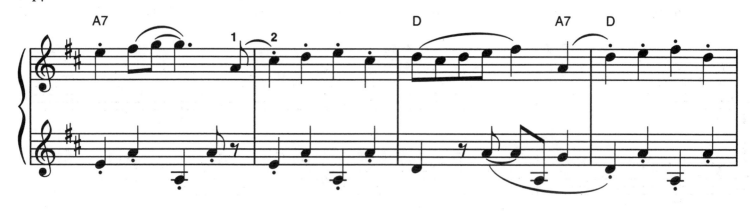

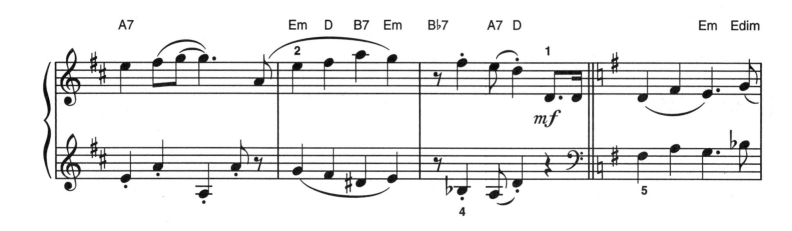

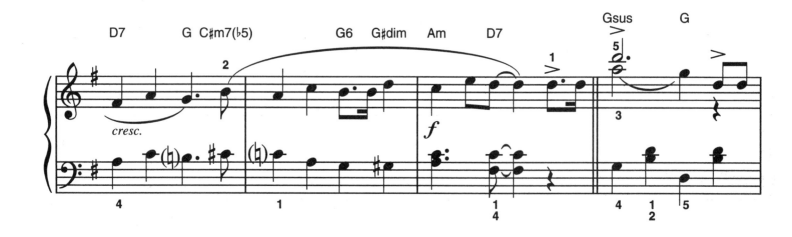

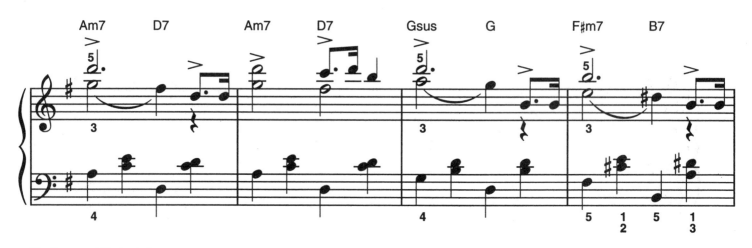

A TRUMPETER'S LULLABY

Arranged by
JOHN BRIMHALL

Music by
LEROY ANDERSON

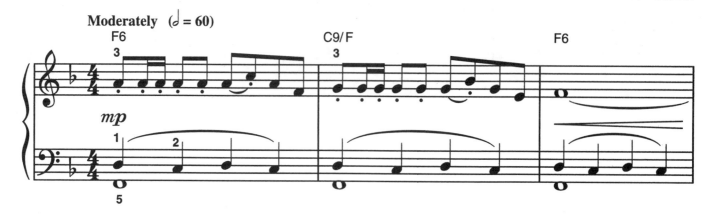

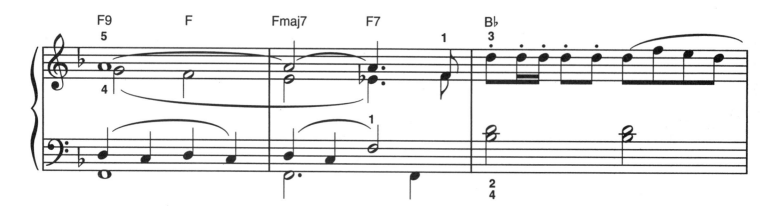

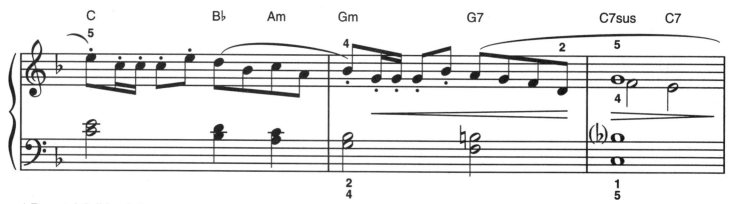

A Trumpeter's Lullaby - 4 - 1

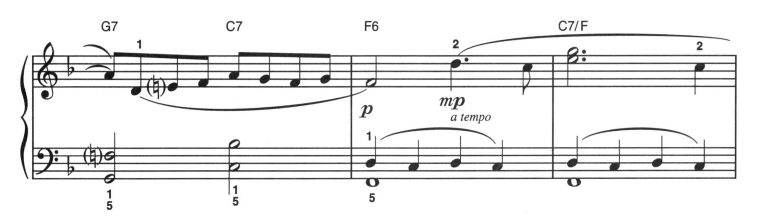

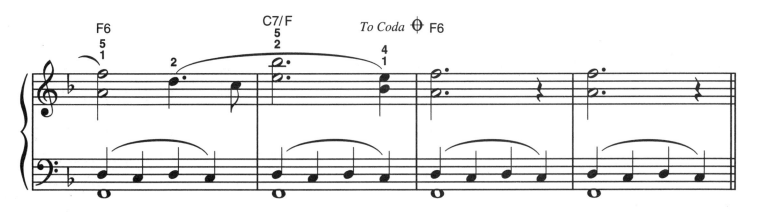

A Trumpeter's Lullaby - 4 - 2

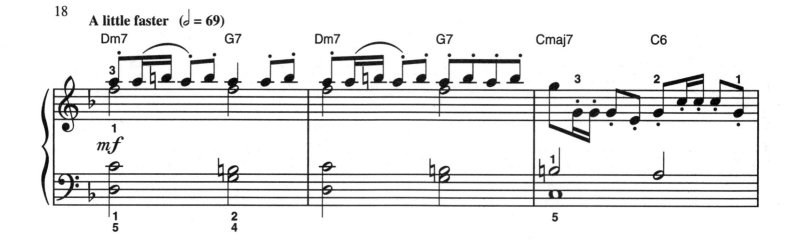

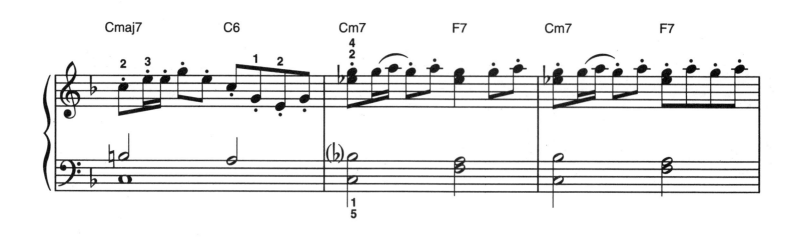

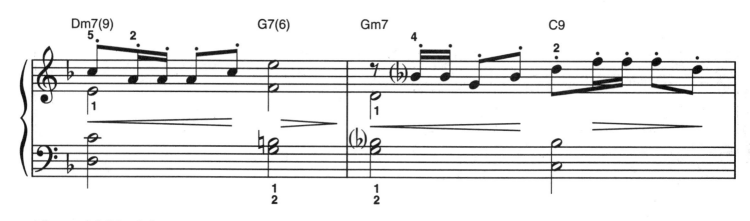

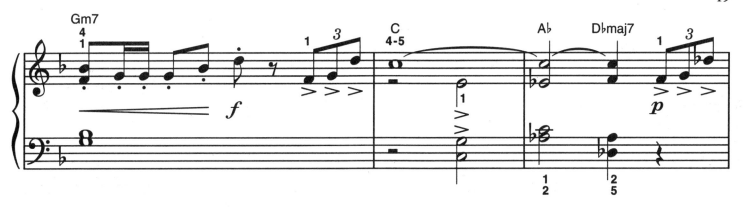

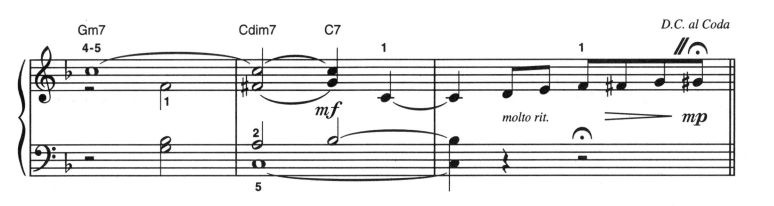

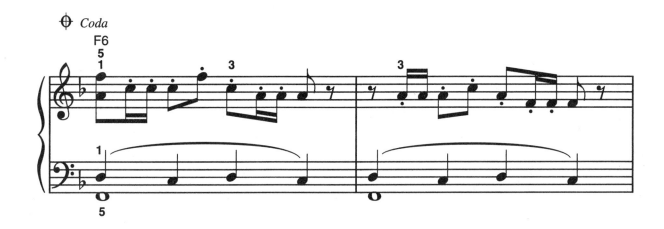

A Trumpeter's Lullaby - 4 - 4

THE WALTZING CAT

Arranged by
JOHN BRIMHALL

Music by
LEROY ANDERSON

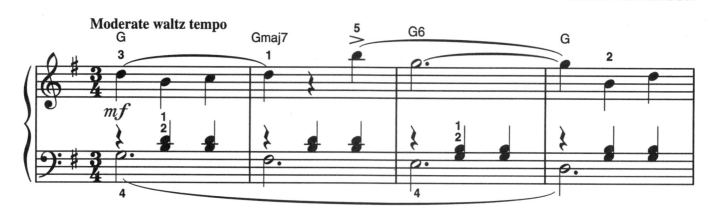

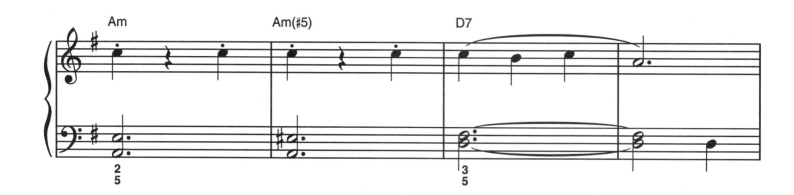

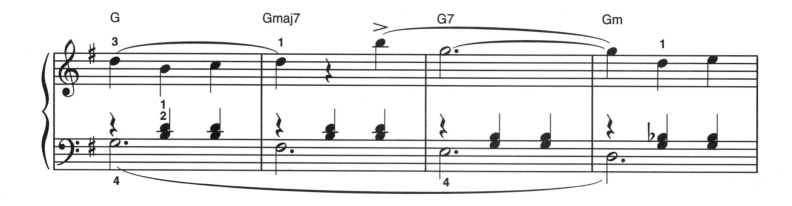

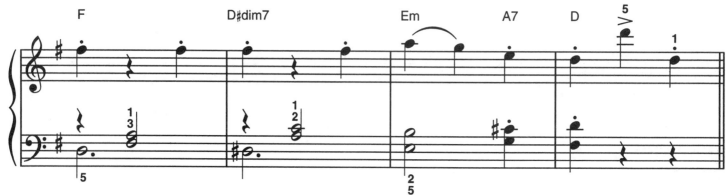

The Waltzing Cat - 4 - 1

FIDDLE-FADDLE

Arranged by
JOHN BRIMHALL

Music by
LEROY ANDERSON

Bright tempo (♩ = 168)

Fiddle-Faddle - 6 - 1

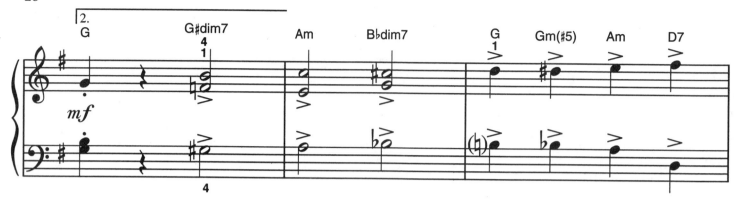

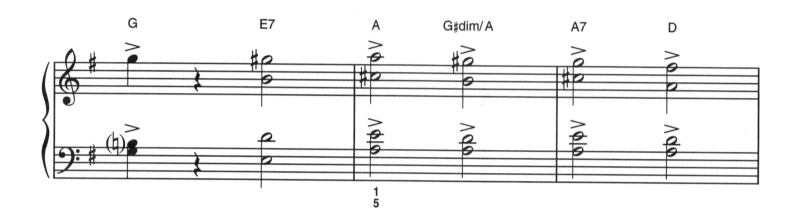

D.C. al Coda II

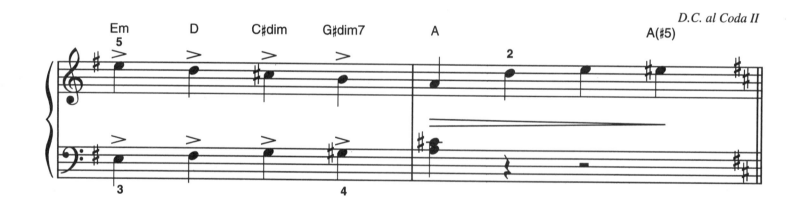

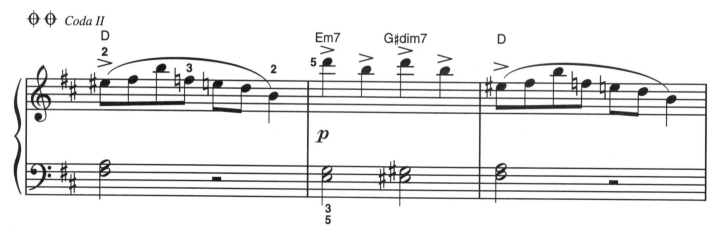

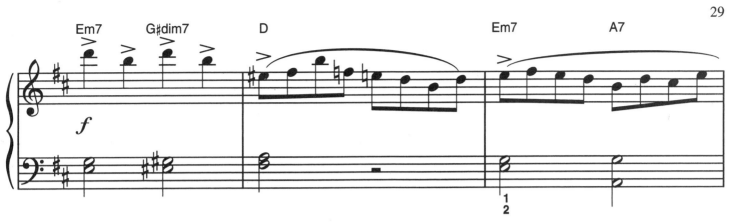

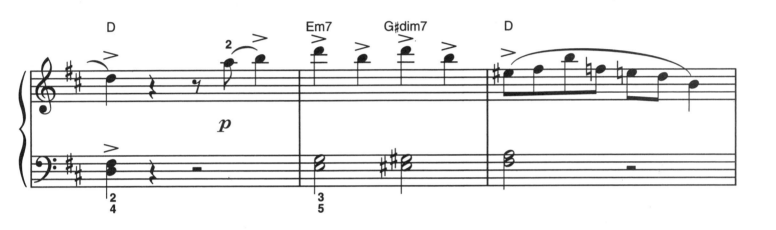

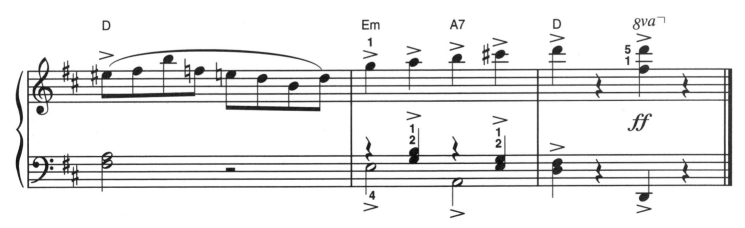

Fiddle-Faddle - 6 - 6

JAZZ PIZZICATO

Arranged by
JOHN BRIMHALL

Music by
LEROY ANDERSON

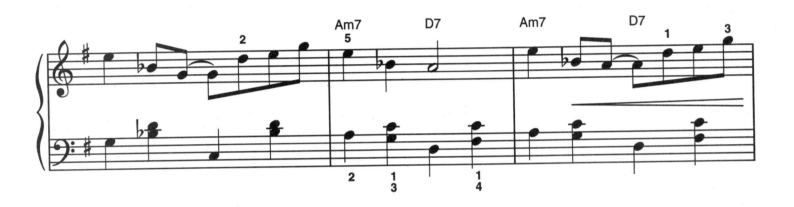

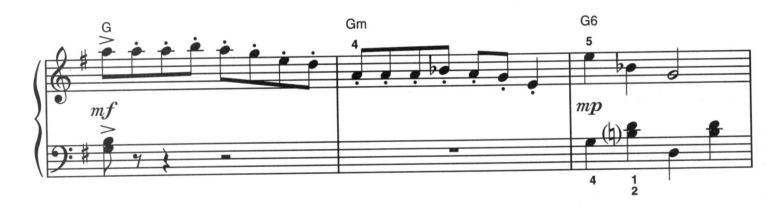

Jazz Pizzicato - 4 - 4

BELLE OF THE BALL
(Waltz)

Arranged by
JOHN BRIMHALL

Music by
LEROY ANDERSON

Bright waltz tempo ($\textstyle\frac{1}{2}$ = 88)

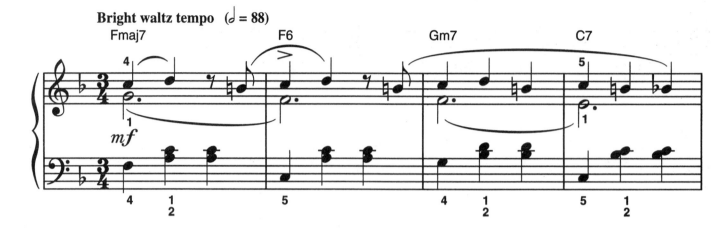

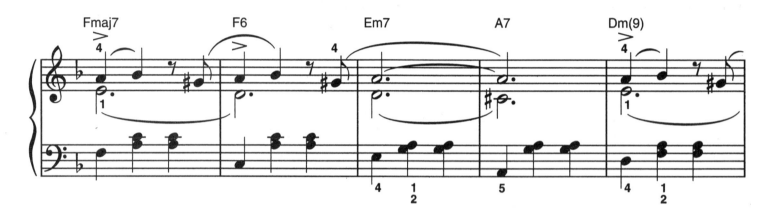

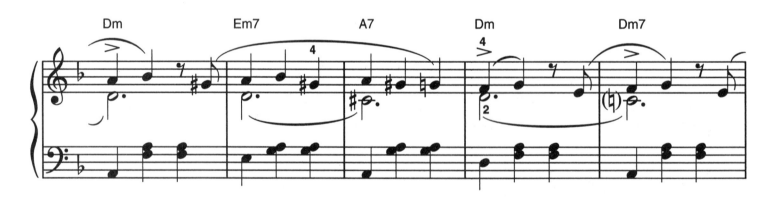

To Coda I ⊕

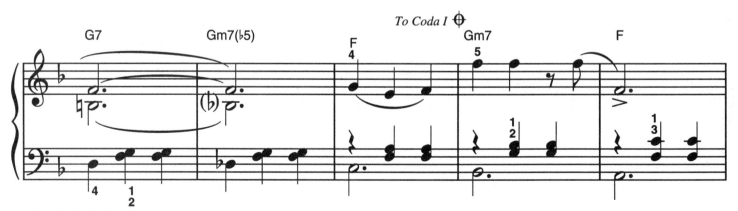

Belle of the Ball - 6 - 1

D.C. al Coda I

⊕ *Coda I*

Belle of the Ball - 6 - 4

BUGLER'S HOLIDAY

Arranged by
JOHN BRIMHALL

Music by
LEROY ANDERSON

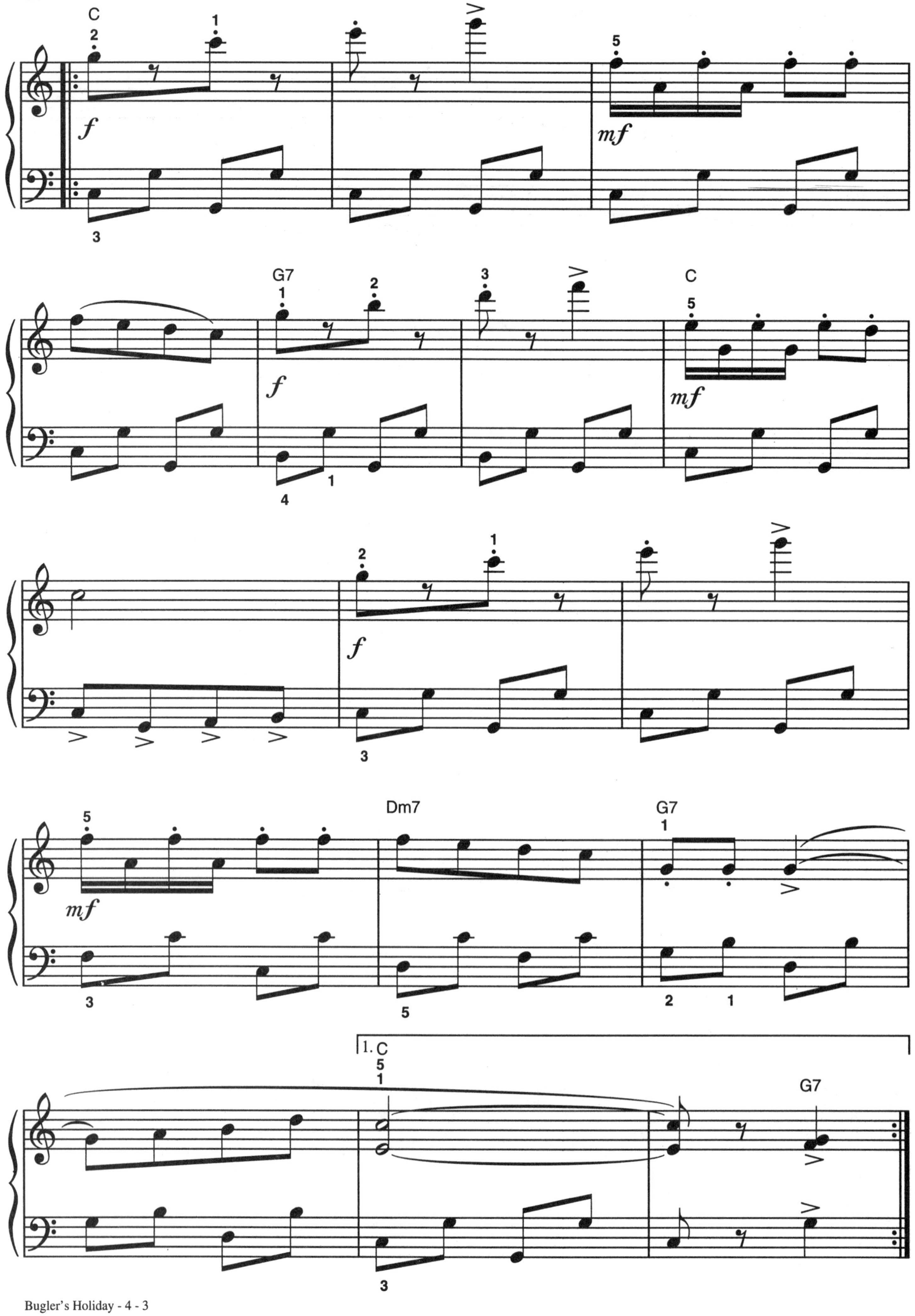
C
f
mf
G7
f
C
mf
f
mf
Dm7
G7
1. C
G7

THE TYPEWRITER

Arranged by
JOHN BRIMHALL

Music by
LEROY ANDERSON

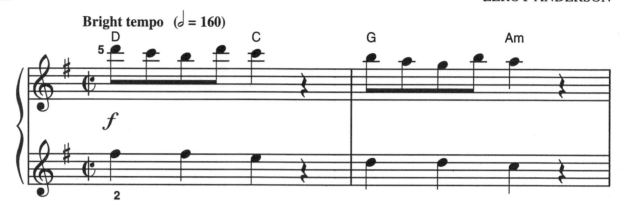

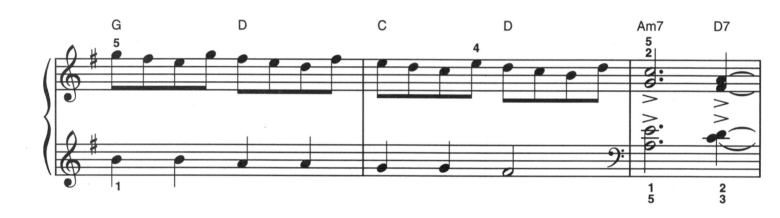

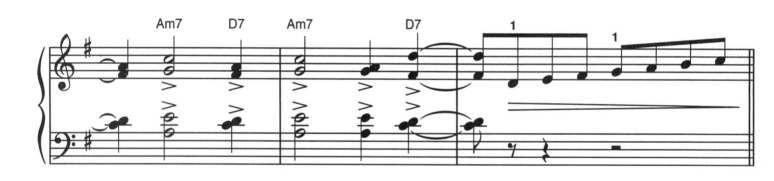

The Typewriter - 6 - 1

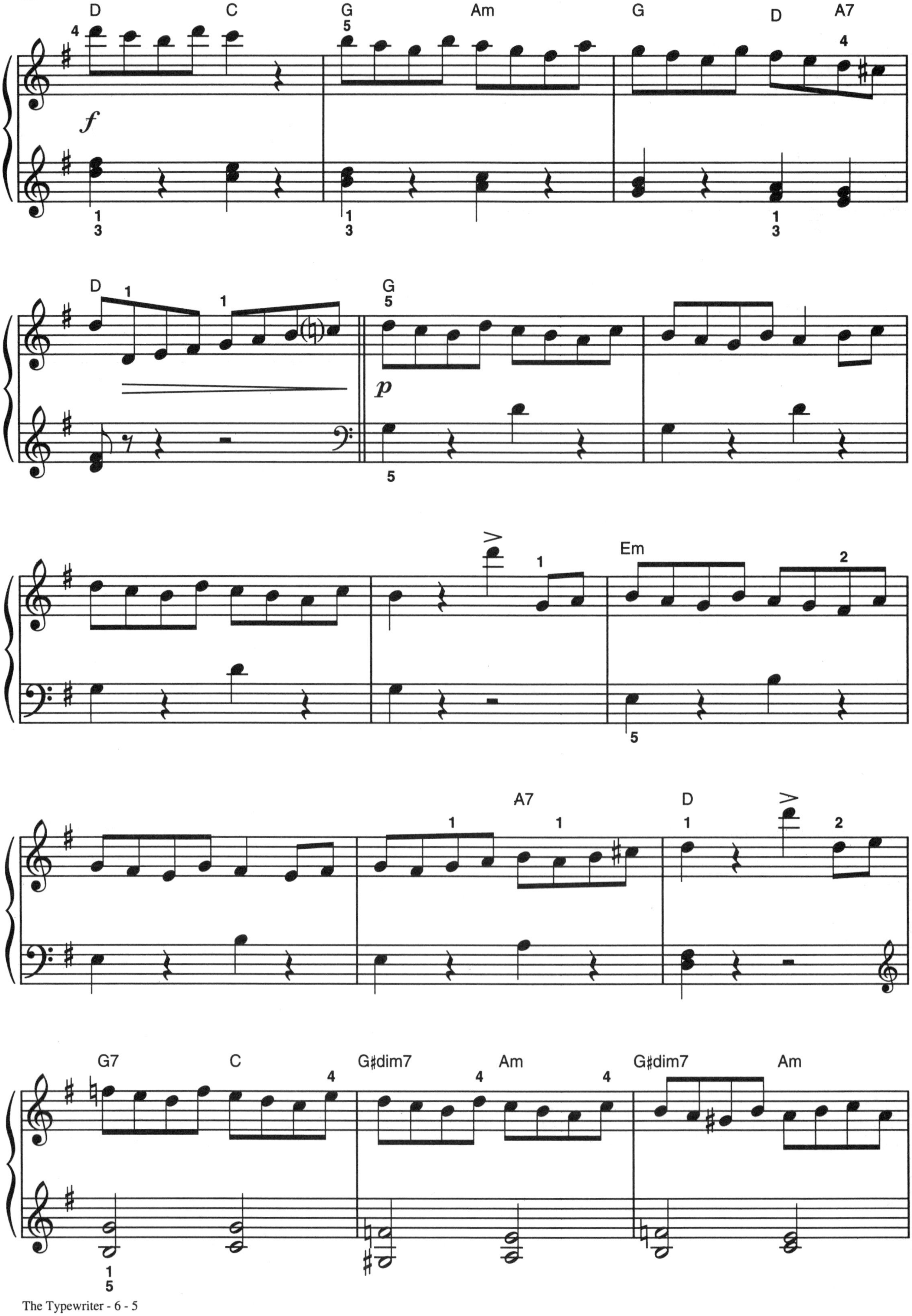
D C G Am G D A7
D G
Em
A7 D
G7 C G♯dim7 Am G♯dim7 Am

The Typewriter - 6 - 6

PLINK, PLANK, PLUNK!

Arranged by
JOHN BRIMHALL

Music by
LEROY ANDERSON

Bright tempo (♩ = 176)

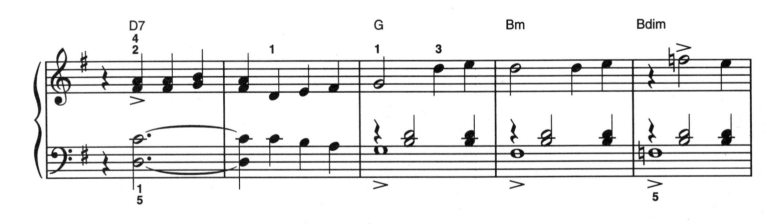

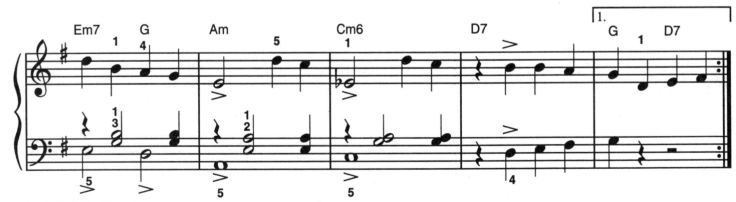

Plink, Plank, Plunk! - 4 - 1

Plink, Plank, Plunk! - 4 - 2

Plink, Plank, Plunk! - 4 - 4

FORGOTTEN DREAMS

Arranged by
JOHN BRIMHALL

Music by
LEROY ANDERSON